PIECES STILL GOOD

A Poetic Reality

JACK ALAN LEVINE

Pieces Still Good
By Jack Alan Levine

Published by Great Hope Publishing, Coconut Creek, Florida

www.Don'tBlowItWithGod.com
www.JackAlanLevine.com
www.LifeSolutionSeminars.com

Contact: Jack@JackAlanLevine.com

Copyright 2015 Jack Alan Levine.
All Rights Reserved. Printed in the United States of America. Except as permitted under United States copyright act of 1976, no part of this publication may be reproduced or distributed in any form, or by any means, or stored in a database retrieval system, without the prior written permission of the copyright holder, except by a reviewer, who may quote brief passages in review.

Neither the publisher nor the author is engaged in rendering advice or services to the individual reader. Neither the authors nor the publisher shall be liable or responsible for any loss, injury, or damage allegedly arising from any information or suggestion in this book. The opinions expressed in this book represent the personal views of the author and not of the publisher, and are for informational purposes only.

Many of the various poems and writings about people in this book draw from real life experience, at certain points involving a composite of people and stories. In some instances people's names have been changed in these poems and writings to protect privacy.

ISBN 978-0-9825526-3-6

PIECES STILL GOOD

CONTENTS

1 INTRODUCTION

5 FLESH WOUNDS

    Just a few excerpts from the mind of
    Jack Alan Levine

54 PHOTOTGRAPHS

59 LIVE AND LEARN

    A poetic collection of modern-day
    expectations, sensations, relations,
    educations, meditations, elations,
    revelations, invitations, and
    undiluted temptations.

INTRODUCTION

As you'll see, I wrote down a lot of poems and thoughts for an entire decade from 1977 through 1987. At the end of that decade I stopped writing poetry. It was an intense time in my life and I used the writings as a way to express my feelings and thoughts and to be able to move on from them by recording the moments as they happened. It was a decade fueled with uncertainty, growth, drug use, heartache and searching. At the end of it my life changed dramatically for the better, I found there was no need to write anymore as I was no longer confused, angry or searching. I had found the key to life and happiness. Life was good. So instead of continuing to write about what was wrong in life… I just took to living and appreciating the good things in life…a very good move on my part!

It is really hard for me to look back on these writings from a time so long past. They begin when I was a young man in college. As I look back, I see the intense feelings I had — the searching, the questions… Who I am? What is life? What's it all about? I see myself going through suffering, pain, growth, realization, breakups with girlfriends, struggles with drug use, as well as trying to figure out what my purpose in life was and what my future was supposed to look like.

Some of what I've written, mostly the drug use parts and some selfish thinking, I find a little embarrassing. All of them were from a time before I came to know Jesus Christ as Lord. Yet I publish them, unedited, because I don't want to leave anything out.
This way you can get a feel for the journey I took to get where I am today.

Seems I was writing a lot from 1977 (my junior year in college) through 1981. Then there's a break in the writings and they pick up again around 1987 when I had back surgery — one of the most intense personal and spiritual growth times of my life. During this time you can see God was extremely prevalent and had a strong influence on me. I look back in amazement as I see how my mind was thinking, how my life was unfolding both good and bad and seeing how God was drawing me closer to Him through all of these "life" circumstances. A few years after this decade of searching ended for me, I accepted Jesus as my Lord and Savior and came to have a personal relationship with God. My life has gotten better every day since then.

As you read, some of the language may be a little harsh, some of the circumstances may be a little frightful, some of the situations may be a little unpleasant, but I can tell you one thing, it was all real! I lived each and every moment of this. I see torment, torture, confusion, frustration, dissatisfaction, fear, greed and a host of other things that were a part of my earlier life. Then I see the transition to a better way of life — a life filled with peace, joy, hope, happiness, mercy, love and kindness — and I am so grateful for that transition.

Of course, I know I had to go through everything I went through to get where I am today and I truly wouldn't trade any of it, although I assure you not all of it was good. I hope that some of the writings and poetry here inspire you, make you think, lift you up, and most importantly serve as an example.
A lot of people look at me today and say, "Jack, you're the happiest guy I know!" And you know what, I am happy. I do have a great life and I'm very grateful for that. But it wasn't always that way. And now you can journey back with me and see firsthand some of my growth…or lack of it (smile!). One thing is certain, you get to see inside of me!

I hope you will want to know how my life turned out after the decade of poem writing ended in 1987. I hope you will fast forward and read the books (not poetry) I've written since then, *Don't Blow It With God*, *Where The Rubber Meets The Road With God*, *Live A Life That Matters For God* and that these books will inspire you greatly and show you the impact and wonderful blessings knowing God and loving God has brought to my life and can bring to yours. That is the true treasure. I also wrote *My Addict Your Addict* a book detailing my battle and victory with drug addiction. For now though, I hope you enjoy this look back on history...scary as it may be!

This book is broken into two sections. The writings from the early years of this book 1977-1981 are titled "Live and Learn." Then the writings from 1987 the year I dealt with crippling back pain and surgery, are called "Flesh Wounds".

I've purposely put the "Flesh Wounds" section first in the book as it's shorter and more intense. Everything I've written has a date on it, but the dates are not in chronological order in the book, also purposely. I've left it in the order I originally arranged it to be read back in those years. I think it gives you a better overall picture...but hey, I've been wrong before...smile!

Anyway...have at it! Remember to look at your own life and by all means, hang on to the pieces that are still good!

Jack Alan Levine

FLESH WOUNDS

Just a few excerpts from the mind of
Jack Alan Levine

TRAITOR

There are traitors everywhere
willing to sell their secrets
for no fee at all
they just get off on being scum.

Trust no one
there are no secrets
except those of the soul.

Frankenstein
took a bride
but she was too beautiful
so she had to hide.
Ugly old frank was out getting a tan
all his friends said
he was quite a man.
The beauty and the beast
the woman and the man.
Go figure.
I still don't understand.

Don't disappoint me.
Even though your airline tickets expired
don't betray your beliefs.
You can still go higher.

FLESH WOUNDS

Car engines
scream and whine.
Sun come out,
hide and then shine.
It's all a lie
the search for the soul…
either it's there
or it's not.

The highway traveler
long since decided
to give up the corporate world.
So he hides away
in plain sight
on the highway.

Indecision
is the death of the mind.
It's the ulcer of the mind —
pure nightmare.
It's better to decide and be wrong
than to suffer the nerve-racking dilemma
and constipation
caused by indecision.

Calmness reigns
after the excitement disappears.
No problem with that
I like calmness.

PIECES STILL GOOD

Can't see the sun.
The shades are closed.
Others put on shades
to block out the sun.

That's like having sex through
a hole in the wall.
Wonder if that's how
the "hole in the wall gang"
got their name.

Miracles
are only the perceptions of individuals.
Must they be documented?
I think not.
It's enough to believe a miracle has occurred.

If people choose
to wrap themselves up in crap (and worry)
then this is their own problem.
I choose to relish (and mustard)
in the glory of the Lord's day
and prosper and delight in the guidance
of his word.

The telephone rings…
another intrusion of my privacy.
But okay
today it's still tolerable.
Tomorrow I will not answer.

FLESH WOUNDS

Worms slither around me,
They slide underneath my feet
and smile in my face.
I chop them in half,
but instead of killing them
I have created two worms
to kill me.
Is this justice
or just God's way of saying
leave the worms alone?

An analysis of the soul is not in order.
An analysis of the ineptitude of the working class
is equally unnecessary.
All analysis is therefore and temporarily
suspended in favor of laughter, joy and friendship.
At this point I suggest you abandon these
writings…in pursuit of the same.

PIECES STILL GOOD

10/12/87
REGRETS

Ah, things change so fast.
I watch as people go from hysterical laughter
to uncontrollable tears.
All in an instant,
all a reaction to a change in environment.

Happenings, events…
the same people
different reactions
depending upon the timing of the event.

It hurts me to share
the painful agonies my friends suffer.
Yet I know they must share it
sometimes though
it makes me think of my own pain and suffering.
That hurts
but I must remember
I have already dealt with my own pain
I have pushed it aside.
In some cases buried it
and in some cases buried it alive.
No need to bring back the dead.

FLESH WOUNDS

Seems like everyone in trouble —
operations, mind games, love.
No one is exempt.

I must remember (as I forget)
not to want for the things
I deemed so meaningless when I faced death's door
and begged the Lord for life
and mercy
so that I may carry His word forward.
Can't forget the promise
or the entire experience
was a useless lie
and then I am only fooling myself.
I can never fool the Lord.

Things like money, jobs, relationships
these are yardsticks we ourselves
use to measure our own worth.
Never are these brought into consideration
when the Lord considers our worth.
Do not be a fool and follow the fools.
Follow your heart to the Lord.

The music on the radio
tells me 'bout blood and guts.
The sportscaster tells me
it was Lendl in two straight sets.
And I tell you, baby,

PIECES STILL GOOD

I've felt a lot of pain
but I have no regrets.

Okay it's time to leave
this computer machine
for another machine
or another thought.
Just remember, Jack,
what's really important
and don't ever,
no never
forget the promise.
And then come judgement day
you'll never,
no never
have any regrets.

FLESH WOUNDS

SUNDAY

Sessions of romance
preceded by sessions of dance.
Her hand in my pants
all from a glance.

Dashing, sophisticated
nothing to fear.
No incest
we are not related.

A city girl
on a country farm,
just a little loving
meant no harm.

Mississippi,
the pride of the South
wedding day
my foot in someone else's mouth.

The whole town was there
brimming with Southern hospitality.
No one even cared
about fate, God or immortality.

PIECES STILL GOOD

But they cared about their farms
and what they called protocol.
So polite… so perfect
stabbing each other in the front
every chance they got.

Glad to leave Mississippi
And see New Orleans
and my guitar-playing friend,
who is only my friend because it was raining.
He's got a record out in Tampa
it's called "nights."
That's nice.
I left when it stopped raining.

The West Coast lady
from the military
still wild as ever
still believes it's necessary.

"Everyone has their own reality,"
says the man from DC.
I don't have to like it,
but I do believe it.

Georgetown, or Baltimore
a snowstorm full of violence.
You know the poor don't steal.
No, they just wait for snowstorms
and loot people like you and me
who were to warm to sit inside.

FLESH WOUNDS

Hey, Ron, yeah you,
with the wife with the blonde hair
that fell to the floor.
Heard from Bobby
she ain't your wife anymore.
You put a shingle outside your house
and that don't mean nothing, brother,
as you found out.

Lecturers, beware!
Your audience is deaf.

I've seen true dedication
and inspiration
in the Southland.
His name is Joe Wheeler.

You think it's tough in Pittsburgh,
no work and families to feed.
My man wheels had it tough
but he never cracked.
That man knows responsibility
you can trust him with your life.
He'd never let you down.
I may not learn responsibility from him
but that's because I don't want to.
But he helped me when everyone else
had long ago packed their bags and left.

A little justice now, hopefully permanent.
Things have changed

and it looks like my man Wheels
got the right end of the deal.
Thanks again, Joe.

I taught a lesson to a young friend
as I explained it to myself.
Simple lesson —
do not bring the past
into present relationships.

You know what you want
in a relationship.
Take it.
Don't confuse it with honesty
and openness.
Today's lesson, boys and girls,
DO NOT MESS UP THE PRESENT
BY BRINGING UP THE PAST!

There is no greater insurance policy than the love of a family. And any premium is worth that love.
If you love your family, take a minute to tell them.

Isn't it absurd how we spend our lives trying to impress strangers who have no concern or care for our well-being. We do nothing or become stupidly complacent about preserving and bonding the love of the people who care for us the most. The worst crime is taking the love of a parent or child for granted. Acknowledge it, revel in it, enhance it

enrich it for all it's worth. It is too late to say,
"I love you," when the casket is laid in the ground.

Once we express a thought, either in writing or
verbally we are free to proceed to the next thought.
Don't keep your thoughts bottled up. They just
grow and then stagnate the area in your brain needed
for new thoughts. Let those thoughts out, even if
it's on paper and nobody sees. Then you are free
to go on to new thoughts. This is the voice of
experience talking.

You ask me, "Jack, how long must I wait for the
guiding hand of the Lord to come and straighten
me out?" You ask me, "Jack, how long must I suffer
before I suffer no more?" And I tell you, "As long as
it takes, my friend. As long as it takes." Looketh to the
Lord now, in your hour of desperation or your hour
of joy. Either to give thanks or ask forgiveness. But
looketh to the Lord for He is where help and salvation
lie. He will watch over you and take care of all His
children. He will hear your voice, and your cup too
shall runneth over with joy.

DAYTIME LAMENT

The old pizza place
has been replaced.
Everywhere I look
I see a new face.

The name of the town
remains the same.
Was everybody related
or just insane?

Don't know how
I would've survived
so many afternoons.
I'll take a bow
cause I've derived
that youth passes too soon.

I have no complaints,
mind you,
I am happy for what is.

I have met many saints
trying to find you
and now I'm ready for kids.

FLESH WOUNDS

It's just so little
but it feels like so much.
I'm too young for Y.A. Tittle
but you're too young to rush
all the philosophers.
They just say the same,
"Poor boy, life is such."

My gram
ninety-one years and going strong.
I don't know who I am
but she knows where she belongs…
close to the soul.

My heart is my home
everything I had
long since blown.
Left here in the wilderness
to face the unknown
and it feels great, just freakin' great,
thanks for asking.

There is an energy released.
There is a spirit captured.
My friends since deceased,
their bodies lie in rapture.
Their worth has increased
now dead for sure.

PIECES STILL GOOD

Those who live on
keep on trying.
Extinct species
and the Third World is dying.

But don't look outside,
you might see it
Close the bedroom door
then you can be it.

Free as a bird
the preacher's word
carries the weight
of others' fate.
Do you remember Larry Tate?

This one's for Randy
who was there when I needed him.
Now that's interesting
cause it makes you wonder
was he in the right place
at the right time
was it some kind of fate?
I don't need an answer.
I really don't mind.
There when I needed him,
Randy's a friend of mine.

All's well that ends well
So I'm ending this well.

FLESH WOUNDS

SOME PEOPLE AIN'T GOT NOBODY

You can look it up, baby
cause that's where it's at.
Some people got nobody
and that's a fact.

Whether they layin'
in some gutter
with an empty bottle
shouting for a brother
who died in battle,

Or maybe they in a king's mansion
dyin' from fatal disease.
Not even a king's ransom
could end the siege.

Yes some got money
and some got brains,
but if you got nobody
you better find someone to blame.

Some got big fancy Cadillac
others got big-money jobs
with no strings attached,
but they scream and beg

PIECES STILL GOOD

to give it all back
if only they could find
their perfect match.

It's a crying shame, darlin'
things end up this way.
I guess it's just the price
a big ego must pay.

So lay down your sorry tune
and open up your arms,
embrace the moon,
and enjoy your lover's charms.
Don't keep it all for yourself.

Your loyalty is earned, not bought.
A thief is rich forever
if he does not get caught.
But don't be caught without a love
or there'll be no one to bring your valuables to you
when that's all you got left to think of.

Yet you can look it up, baby,
because that's where it's at.
Some people got nobody
and that's a fact.

FLESH WOUNDS

10/10/87
5 A.M.
NO LOVE HERE

      I know you didn't love me.
      Well I didn't love you either
      but I knew someday
      we'd both be believers.

      Playin' those silly games
      you know, the emotional kind...
      if this ain't a sin, baby,
      you won't wind up blind.
      I don't care what you do to your head
      but please don't mess up mine.

      It's been a long time, baby
      since we sang the same song.
      It ain't crime,
      but it sure is wrong.

      So go ahead, darlin'
      and do what you do.
      I'm ten times better
      since I'm rid of you.

PIECES STILL GOOD

No more of your nagging
and your hind feet draggin'
you always hated my success
said I was just bragging.

Sorry what I sung
wasn't for you
gifts that I brung
were never yours too.

I hope you get a second chance
with some sucker from the West.
Tell them how you like to dance
and put him to the test.
Turn off the lights
he can't see the truth in the dark.
Don't tell about your bite
it's much worse than your bark.

It's all over, baby,
and that's for sure.
No amount of money
can bring me back for more.

Soon it will be Halloween
and then it's trick or treat.
Just fade into the sunset
and pour me Jack Daniel neat.
There's nothing wrong with trying
as long as you can live with the defeat.

FLESH WOUNDS

10/14/87
EASY

(This is called EASY because it was an easy name to think of)

Well we can jump off the bridge
but the river's much to cold.
The nautical winds
that blow the sailor home
are all confused
and the watchmen in the watchtower
are all drunk and stoned.
There's a lot of women
just now, learnin' to live alone.

Now don't get disgusted
at the suggestions of the doctor.
Don't get distressed
at the banker's success.

Picture frames
preserve memories.
Doctors, saints
cure disease.
But even ice
cannot the heart freeze

destined to be bewildered
by that fatal, lovesick disease.
Bring even Hercules
down to his knees.

The snow covered mountains
that I slide down
are nothing compared
to commando raids
made upon my heart and soul.

The milkmen
do the same every day
just like the mailmen
who count their weekly pay.
Both have something
yes something to say
but somehow it gets lost
washed away
in the sameness of their lives.
Who knows
what the future holds
or what tomorrow brings.
He who sings now
sings best.
He who waits to sing
is an idiot.
You can quote me on that.

FLESH WOUNDS

Subterranean lifestyles
too deadly for me
so much carbon monoxide
make it too cloudy to see.

A letter from a friend
warms my bones.
In two short weeks, baby,
I'm going home.
But I am home now.
Give that to a physics or logic major to figure out…
it's easy.
I have two homes
and I've always said,
"Two homes are better than one."

All confusion
is unraveled for me
on a need-to-know basis
with God as the key.
Any disillusion
cannot the physic woman dispel
enter God's kingdom of heaven
or rot in hell.

Sundown
on summertime land,
bright rainbows
and visions
of the holy land.

PIECES STILL GOOD

The migrant farmer
and the good old boy banker
exist in peaceful respect.
They both understand
that in order to live
you gotta share the land.

Don't be fooled by con men
who wear the cloth.
Cloth does not the soul make
the soul is what it is.
Open it up and examine it.
Do not accept the doctor's diploma as proof of competency.
Do not accept the preacher's cloth as proof of faith.
Demand to see the skill,
the work, the truth, the faith
of any man who claims to be the son of God.

FLESH WOUNDS

NOT FUNNY

Holy smoke
it ain't no joke
invisible things
eating up the universe
the father and son
sit and drink beers
while the mother and the daughter
knit and curse.

War veterans
with bottles of Excedrin
take the oath of their country
and lay it aside

pull out their old uniforms
missing all the buttons
start braggin'
bout the USA pride.

But memories fade
and peacetime eases tension.
The vets old and gray
now live on government pension.

PIECES STILL GOOD

But there's a new war coming
and that's for sure.
Too old for running,
the vet can't fight anymore.

The old warrior
yeah, that one.
He's real happy now
they just drafted his son.

Forget that proud look.
War sucks.
It's no fun to die.

Your bathroom may be dirty
but your name is clean,
and in the end, brother,
that's what it all mean.

FLESH WOUNDS

TENDER MOMENTS

Tender moments long gone,
muddy waters cloud the sky.
There is light in the sky
but no tunnel to dig.
You need an explanation, for what?
For terror, for fear, for hope?

Is there courage left anywhere?
Where is the escape clause?
The sparrow who long ago left the nest
is now lost somewhere in the southland.

Whoever said you can't go home again was wrong.
You can go home again
but you must get sick, very sick.

My friend tells me he goes without sleep.
He is distraught, caught and bought
but swears he has Ghandi-like energy
escorting him through these sleepless days.
Unfortunately he is not Ghandi.
He collapses, tired and depressed
still not knowing the secrets of the Indian god
for he is only human, more human than most.

PIECES STILL GOOD

Opportunity comes in many forms
I am bedridden,
but instead of being depressed
I lay enlightened.
For the first time in years I am able to reflect,
to pause, to think
and listen to the voice of my soul.

I can change direction
or keep moving forward,
but I have the choice and chance to shape my future.

I have an experience money cannot buy.
I have conversed and shared the soul of many
all of whom I would have never seen
under any circumstances but these.

I have shared insight into my family
that I certainly would have missed
had I continued to live in this whirlwind existence
I had created for myself.

An existence that would have satisfied me
until death,
but now I get a chance, a gift
a vision, a renaissance
a rebirth, a trial.

I have been laid up and out
yet I do not bask at my misfortune
for I quickly realized this was no misfortune.

FLESH WOUNDS

But rather a necessary, helpful experience
that will benefit me the rest of my life.
Not meant to hurt, shorten or take away from my life
but to add, enhance and enlighten my very existence
and to open up my very soul.

I saw the woman
who captured my heart.
Together we played,
hugged,
memories of our love
swept through our hearts.
It was wonderful to see her again.

I do love her.
I delight in her happiness.
We shared our souls
bared our hearts
our minds still lie to each other
not to trick the other
but to prevent the tears.

Leaving open the doors to the future
is security for both of us.

The scary moments
of modern medicine miracles
are nothing except fleeting moments of fear.
Man is on the moon.
Surgery is routine.
We can repair and replace hearts.

PIECES STILL GOOD

We can reattach limbs
and reconstruct organs of the body.
Our worries are only for our own mortality
for the technology is solid
as long as the doctor is sober.

The holy man he cometh
like the newspaper delivery man
on time, everyday
with spiritual greetings
that are ignored by everyone
except those who need them.

It only takes one time
to appreciate the holy man
to attach yourself to him
in the hope he will attach you to God.
That might work, but
you are better off having prior attached yourself to God.
Then you will not have to depend on anyone
holy or otherwise
to save your soul and your body.

In order to survive you must employ
one of the following two elements —
faith or humor.
Preferably, ideally, you have both.

FLESH WOUNDS

My new theory on life is simple:
one ought never complain unless you are
on the operating table.
Anything else
is merely an event in your life,
an event, which in the final end,
will be rendered irrelevant by history.
The biggest crime is worrying ourselves
over anything at this very moment that may
eliminate or substitute for the joy of this moment.

I get a letter from my friend, a female,
Far away in the west.
Too much danger out there in the west,
people shooting each other on the highway
for no reason at all.

She's having trouble remaining faithful.
Is anyone faithful anymore?
Only you are faithful, Lord.

PIECES STILL GOOD

VIENNA, VIETNAM, VICTIMS AND VICTORY

I am in New York in October
and it's cold.
One hour north it's snowing
and my brother is trapped in Ghent, New York.
Not a Domino's Pizza in sight.
Soon the snow will turn to rain
and my brother will be home, safe again.
Is this too great a price to pay
only for those who choose New York to stay?

My best friend, Dynamite Dave "Tank" Murry Fortunoff
and I both know Vienna is the place to go.
We have convinced ourselves
with a little help from Billy Joel
that Vienna is indeed a state of mind
and we can obtain it.

Vietnam veterans,
the ones I see now
both publically and privately
seem to be getting it back together.
They have organizations

and it appears have readjusted
to life here in America.

You don't see or hear much these days
about your Vietnam vet flip out or killing rampage.
I guess some are locked away
in hospitals or jails
and many have accepted the injustice of war.
Even though they may never forget it
and it remains part of them every waking hour,
they have learned to stop talking about it.

People are only interested in tragedies
when they happen. It took the Vietnam vets a
decade to return to the graces of their country.
Better late than never. But nobody said there
was justice. Just a reminder while we are on
the subject of justice…you should always take
your justice wherever and whenever you can get it!

My eyes are roaming. Looking around modern-day
America as we know it in 1987, I am seeing more
victims than ever. The poor are victimized by their
neighbors as they suffer percentagewise from the
highest number of violent crimes. The young are
victimized by the young and old alike as they are
raped physically, and then the country rapes
them of an education, their parents rape them
of a good upbringing and loving home and eventually
they become rapists. I'll pause to acknowledge this is

PIECES STILL GOOD

a broad generalization, but I'll leave it anyway. The elderly are victimized by the devaluation of their dollars if indeed inflation has not raped them of all their dollars in the first place. The old are subject too and victimized by a rapidly deteriorating healthcare system that is tangled in a web of bureaucracy and has long ago abandoned its number one purpose ... quality healthcare, in favor of everyone's number one purpose ... profit. Perhaps Ted Kennedy is the only hope for the old and for the young who before they know it will be old. Good citizens with a solid constitution are victimized by organized crime, which has come out of the saloons and off the docks onto the neighborhood streets and into your living room. Honesty is no longer the best policy, for like many beautiful and worthwhile things, it too is extinct.

Victory, while most prevalent in sporting arenas and politics is also commonplace in war and business. But that kind of victory is a victory for an entity, either the country, corporation, political party or sports team. Here's the good news ... there is still individual victory to be obtained. We are our own judges and we alone can determine our victories. Victory to you may be visiting a sick friend in the hospital, helping an old person across the street, donating money to the North Shore Animal League or making sure an elderly or indigent person does not get treated badly by a nasty restaurant employee. Victory may be awakening and relishing the fact that you have awoken and are alive to breathe. It might be a job well done or knowing that somebody loves you. I just want to know one thing — how come these things start out as poems and wind up as dissertations in the middle? I'm probably just too lazy to care about spacing when I'm thinking. Hmm?

You know this New York is one cold city.
It's October 5th and it's starting. Get your snow shovels and winter coats. Not me and the Pup, the only thing we are getting is out of here just as soon as I am able.

The world is crazy, if we let it, incidents and circumstances will drive us insane or cause us to worry to death. Remember you are who you are whether it is raining or the sun is shining. Whether you are the head of a company or the busboy in the cafeteria. My old man told me a long time ago, "They can't take away your mind unless you let them." Don't you let them. Don't you.

ETERNITY

Mirror images
of ourselves
and still
no satisfaction.

Break your back
but they put your head
in traction.

Instant cure
modern medicine
and you're back in action.
Oops…misdiagnosis
and you're dead.
Less pain when you're dead.

Weather changing
life changing
people changing,
Aside from that
everything stays exactly the same.

Bad directions
bad selections
and everything you built

FLESH WOUNDS

crumbles like sand
and all the beautiful music
disappears with the band.
They're busted for possession
of the music.

They're thrown in jail
but the cops keep the evidence
and we lose the music.

Go ahead pop the cork.
Holy crap, they defeated Bork.
There's a case of a genius
having to look like an idiot
to convince idiots
that indeed, he too is an idiot
so they have nothing to fear.
He succeeded
everyone is convinced he's an idiot.

The only true trusts
are those not defined by words
but known by souls.

Enter the new day
Fearless
Untroubled by yesterday's anger
Here, to take it's own turn at bat.

Enter the new baby
fearless

unknowing of yesterday's agony.
Good luck.

Enter the sorrow of yesterday
into the adult of today
causing him to throw away
the very best of times
his crime.
For it's his time.
Don't you make mistake
that is the same.

Clean your closets
and throw away the crap.
Then clean your soul
and throw away the crap.

TV is a joke
so only watch what's funny.
Educate your children by yourself.
better teachers cost more money.
Do not let others dictate
right from wrong.
Do not let others decide
what is best for your child.
Take the responsibility, take the blame
take the hassle, take the shame.
In the long run you will be glad…
too much at stake.

FLESH WOUNDS

When anything of importance is entrusted
to the idle, futile hands of others,
the only ones to trust
the fathers, mothers, sisters and brothers.

The shadows they sit
with the losers
whose souls have quit
next to the piles
of the mongrel mutts crap
They perfectly fit
All of them
soon to be lit
by sunlight or alcohol.

The depression that waits
until opportune time
a California earthquake
a New York city street mime
sooner or later it all ends.
You take yours
and I'll take mine.

Dave (Murry, "Tank") and I have decided
to leave all our doors open
and walk only through the ones we want to,
but Tank asks
what happens
if all the doors are closed.
I tell him,
"Find new doors."

PIECES STILL GOOD

The washing machine
spins round and round
to clean dirt from clothes.
The earth
spins round and round
to clean dirt
from living souls.

Breadsticks for breakfast
get your kicks
while they last.
The old folk tell me
it ends much too fast.
The punk rockers say
it better, to do it all fast.
The warlords say
end it with a blast
and the parents cry
when the flag be half mast.
The music in my ears
reflects my tears
or sometimes the happiness
of my heart.
I choose not to pull apart
the dreams that I start.

I'll love you forever
if I so choose
because that's what I really want to do.
If my love not be returned

FLESH WOUNDS

I do not lose
cause I love to sing the blues.
I hate the Post and the Daily News
but in the end
everyone walks in their own shoes.
The lesson of this verse is
make sure your shoes are comfortable
because in the end, YOU
and only YOU,
will be walking in them.

The motion picture show
and the black preacher
with nowhere to go
each tell me
there's something I must know.
The preacher,
the teacher
and my so-called friend
all tell me they know
where I should go.
But Santa Claus, he knew best
when he told them all
ho, ho, ho.

Desperation does not scare me.
Neither do crashing airplanes.
Both of them amaze me
as I try to decipher what is truly sane.
Is it sunshine? Is it rain?

PIECES STILL GOOD

Is it pleasure? Is it pain?
Or is there a fine line
that balances all of it
controlled by the brain?

And now you wonder
just who to blame.

I enjoy the daytime
and the peaceful night.
I've enjoyed a lot lately
as I increase my sight.
Sometimes you can be surrounded by less
and see more.
It's all in your attitude
got nothing to do with vitamin,
nutrition or food.

My friends,
smile.
"It's life and life only."
Ain't that right, Bobby?

FLESH WOUNDS

DAY BEFORE

Doctors saving lives
with their textbooks
and their knives.

People ruining souls
both men and wives.
They call it cheating
but that's not it.
I call it beating,
beating each other's brains out.

Gee, marriage is joyous
pain, sorrow and crisis
out of all I've seen.
Ken and Barbie
have been the nicest,
they could not walk
and they could not talk

The motorcycle mama
who dumped me off her bike
made me stretch like a lama
to see what I liked.

PIECES STILL GOOD

She said,
"Boy, I assure you,
you are no highway man."
I said, "Mama,
you must be crazy
cause you just don't understand."

Walking the halls
looking for the answers
none exist in the halls
only bare cold and white paint
on the walls.
Locked apartments
where people live and hope falls
even though destiny calls.
It can't get in
there are "Do Not Disturb" signs
on every door.
Do not disturb what?

My mountain retreat
has no heat
but it's the warmest place I know.

It's where I am
when I don't know who I am.
It's where I am
when I'm exactly sure of just that.
It's where I am, where you are not.

FLESH WOUNDS

It erases nothing
but I already forgot.

The bears in the woods
they do not fear me,
they do not scare me,
they share the woods with me.
They eat my garbage
and I lock my door.
That's a fair deal.

I'll do the rest from here, Lord.
Just knowing you're there is enough for me.
You and only you
can wipe away the sin.
Thanks for being my eraser.

The man with the evil eyes
is a profit.
He hides behind his eyes
for if he shows his cards,
he's sure someone will knock them down.
Or else he fears he may drop them.
In this case he is justified to hide.

Midnight is but another hour on the clock
with no significance whatsoever
either spiritual or emotional.
Live each hour as if it were your last.
Be sure to enjoy it.

PIECES STILL GOOD

The winners and the losers
separated only by defeat,
the obedient dog
subservient
is stuck
with the cruelty of human expectation.
Three cheers for the cat.

Episodes of happiness
events that take up our time
and our days
soon pass,
leaving us back at square one,
which is back with ourselves.

The moon tonight scares me not.
Life is merely a monopoly board
you go round and round
and only when the game is over
do you realize where you have landed.

The highway worker
on the chain gang,
he is content
for his day is decided.
The businessman
with the ulcer,
he is frustrated
for he faces with uneasy nervousness
each day, each meeting, each second
judged only by his last performance.

FLESH WOUNDS

Treasures
buried under the sea
do not tempt me.
Smiles to be shared and given,
these tempt me
for these I would steal.
They are the true treasures.

There is no feeling
quite as satisfying
as doing something for someone
unasked, with no reward in mind
and none given.
Try it.

The paintings on the wall
stare at me.
I blow them off
they are stuck there.

The end of the line comes quickly
for those who do not walk it.
The language and its meaning
goes away quickly
for those who do not talk it.

Anyway it's afternoon
and afternoons are great
although they are like the newness of morning,
they do not carry the finality of night time.

PIECES STILL GOOD

The gray sky
has no answer
to the victims' plea.
I have not the answer.
What you get
is what you see.

Me and "Baltimore Bob" Kurland, at the time no doubt the smartest man I ever met.

Old girlfriend Brenda, one of three old girlfriends I write about in this book. She broke my heart, but it was well worth it!

College buddies: (standing), Bruce Damon, Scott "Space" Brainerd and Me, (sitting) Rick Sands and Puppy, at the time by far the greatest dog ever to live!

College Buddies: (left to right), Scott "Space" Brainerd, Me, Barry Kleckner, "Baltimore Bob" Kurland and Rick Sands, who by the way had girls crawling all over him at all times, we all benefited from the overflow!

This picture was painted in my junior year in college at Syracuse University by an art student who lived in my building named Lee Boot. I paid him $50.00 bucks to paint it as a birthday present for my mother. Turns out Lee Boot went on to become a well known artist. Nice to know I got his career started...smile!

This picture of me was taken in the back seat of Leo Harmonay's car by my friend John Rizzo, another college buddy. Turns out Rizzo became a very celebrated photographer. Glad I could give him his big break...Smile!

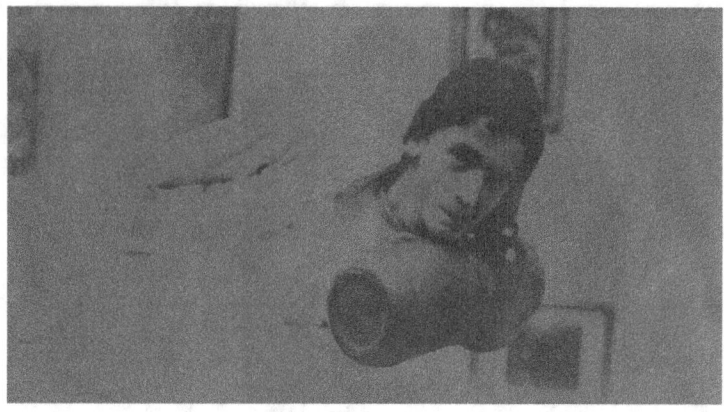

This picture was another one John Rizzo took of me. Somehow he has me floating in the air, or maybe I was floating in the air. Not quite sure. what I am sure of is I used to wear that beanie hat a lot in Syracuse because it was always cold. I know I only wrote stuff down when it seems I was upset or searching, but there are a ton of great times in college as you can clearly see by the pictures!

It's unbelievable we got to live like this! Sophomore year in college 1976. What a great year, tapestries on the wall, guitars, headbands, life was good.I wasn't such a great guitar player but I really loved playing and writing original stuff. And what the heck, at least I looked the part.

That's my puppy Roy. We snuck him into the dorm where we lived at Syracuse University. He was a great guy, very cute and attracted lots of girls!!! I had him for 2 months. He had worms. So after 2 months of worms in our dorm room and neighbors telling us to "shut that dog up" we were fortunate enough to find a local girl who lived on a farm who would take him and Roy lived happily ever after. Loved having spent some time with the Roy man! Doesn't get any better than a boy and his dog.

LIVE AND LEARN

A poetic collection of modern-day expectations,
sensations, relations, educations, meditations,
elations, revelations, invitations, and
undiluted temptations

LIVE AND LEARN

5/26/81
10.45 P.M.
(FINAL EDITING SESSION)

> Those of you
> who have this book
> have in your hands
> my most valuable possession-
> *-my thoughts-*

Life is good now and it makes me very happy to be able to feel this way. So take whatever you need from this book and leave the rest behind, and then…on with the living.

Love,
Jack

PIECES STILL GOOD

The Lord lets us laugh.
We'd be fools to cry.

LIVE AND LEARN

9 / 9 / 8 1

Every day —
Seems like a night time
Any day —
Seems like the right time

Flowers surround the grass
moonbeams in the afternoon
we walkin' on sanded glass
surrounded by rainbows —
not a moment too soon

Is everything real?
or just some far-away land
any secrets left to conceal
leave them with the band…

stained shadows..
of yesterday gone by
powers that be, sustained
sit up high
but they all must look up…
to see me eye to eye.

PIECES STILL GOOD

5 / 1 2 / 8 1

Can you hear me now, damned if this isn't a desperate boy talking now. Things moving along at no pace at all. I'm moving but I'm weepin'. But that weep should be long gone by now.

Can you feel me now? Are you there? You must be. You must help me now more than ever. Hey I'm back to you, remember when it happened before, only the name was different. She said, "No more. Don't come back here no more." And I said, "I don't believe this. You can't send your lover home." She said, "That's right, but you ain't my lover, so please leave." And I left, limped away weakly, meekly, timid under the sky. But those days are gone and new days arose. Now I'm faced with the same dilemma, and Lord put a pillow under my head cause I've hit bottom. Only one way up, that's to the top, Lord. Pick me up, stand me forthright and I swear together we'll fight till life's end.

Don't need no saviors, just need strength, guidance, deliverance, substance. You are master of all creatures, Lord, and that includes her. Therefore there must be reason for her actions,

and they must be your reasons. I'll never fault
that although I might not understand it.

Yes I'm pleading to you, Lord. Lead me by the
hand, help me understand, just get me through.
I'm not sure that I want to understand anyway.
You've given me everything a boy could ask for
in life, and yes, I do mean everything. Sometimes
things leave so suddenly, and only you know why.

Lord, guide me, slide me through this sticky
wasteland my mind is glued to. Just take me
away from it, and I'll make it through. Leave
me here, even better, to face it. Because, boy,
if you can face this one, you'll understand.

You see the universal sign of the oneness of the
mind, that lets us walk blind, because we know
the direction. Stay and fight this one, boy.
Then we can share the victory joy. Faith is all
you need, justice will be served. Sometimes it
hurts to watch them bleed, but, man, that blood sure
do it pour out, it do.

My blood is flowing, and yes, I'm knowing the pain
that can lead up to the sky. I guess I'd be a
fool to question it or dare to define it. I must
live within the confines of the premises or I can't
live. I can't escape from the being that I am,
nor do I seek to. Reduction of the pain is the
primary goal, but is there really pain? Am I

PIECES STILL GOOD

really suffering? And if so is it as severe as
I make it? Has it not already been inscribed
many months ago, has it not been placed clearly
before me. Only I kept saying, "No." Really
that is the truth. Now I must accept the reality
before me for just what it is, and thank the Lord
I am strong enough to face the reality fate
has placed before me, whether I agree or not,
like it or not. I must accept it and do my part
to live for the Lord, and he will do his part
for me.

You see, I even must wish well for my former
love, and for her present love. For they are
loving under the eyes of the Lord and their
love is blessed, just as mine was and always will
be. May there be eternal happiness, justice
and many smiles for you, for me, and for all those
you cherish and love. Even Springsteen suffers.
Bob Marley's dead and the police are baffled in
Atlanta. Me, I'm walkin' along in the spirit of
the Lord. How can any man, white or black ask
for more than that? Thank you, Lord.

LIVE AND LEARN

1981

> Betrayed by my own innocence
> incensed by my betrayal
> strangled,
> by the stronghold of my faith
> faithfully waiting to be free.

PIECES STILL GOOD

1981

I'm sailing on the Lord's ship, on the Lord's
waters. It is His course that guides me, His
It is He who sets my final direction.

He steers me clear of troubled waters and
prevents me from developing leaks in the bow
of my ship. If per chance I stumble carelessly,
He gently picks me up, pats me on the back
and reminds of His will.

It is to Him I bequest my heavenly existence
here on this earth. It is with His help I will
do the most, best, good for mankind. If He
chooses to test my love or loyalty for Him, He
will see that it is eternal.

I have many faithful and loyal friends, lovers
and companions, all, however, are susceptible to
changing their mind at any time and withdrawing
their friendship, love and companionship.

LIVE AND LEARN

The Lord, on the other hand, will never let
go of His love for me, and I return His love
wholeheartedly.

Sometimes I need to be reminded of my ultimate
destiny and this old rat trap world seems
to get me caught up in its tangled web of fog,
making it hard to see clearly and impossible to
see what's ahead.

I'm okay though, I'm okay. All the instrument
panels may be down, but my navigator (the Lord)
is with me forever.

PIECES STILL GOOD

3/31/77

A great philosopher once said to me,
"Son, it only takes one light to see."

A great truck driver was sitting on his rig
said, "Son, it only takes one shovel to dig."

A great butcher was cutting his meat
said, "Son, you need two to call them feet."

A great carpenter was sawing his wood
said, "Son, I'm going to heaven."
I wondered if he could.

A great president was sitting by his seal and
said, "Son, it only takes one button
to make the whole damn thing real."

LIVE AND LEARN

12/23/80

>Misunderstood
>Misdirected
>Murdered
>Resurrected
>
>Back again
>smiling this time
>remember when
>I walked the line
>
>Well I don't walk nowhere
>now for nobody
>don't do nothin'
>for anybody
>
>Times have changed
>good to bad
>and thankfully
>back again
>
>Seeing the strangers
>ain't so bad
>at least they don't
>have preconceived
>notions

PIECES STILL GOOD

you can still mold
their shapeless emotions
yeah shapeless emotion is where it's at

I'm a dreamer, Shakespeare,
but you, you're a writer
all I'm asking for I have
already received
everything from here on in
is just a present

There is no justice
no service
only the Lord's will!

LIVE AND LEARN

7 / 1 4 / 8 0

The inspiration
reaches out
of the realm
of the atmosphere

the invitation
bleaches out
the helm
by the peer

The fisherman in murky waters
fish blood on his hands

the astronaut
the mortician
buried in the mud
in the outer space of the land

the highway
and the housewife
both victim of circumstance
wonder if religion
can salvage the wallflowers' dance.
Is there salvation in dance?

PIECES STILL GOOD

Racy movies
and French woman
black hair
and dark skin

white faces
snow-blind places
don't need cold weather
to leave Eskimo traces

Trampoline, kerosene
I believe
in meat that's lean
eat that!

Time will pass
us by!
When was the happiest?
perhaps when I saw
that man
definitely not when the sun
was shining

Gray skies and rain
can be the two most
beautiful things
be they void of pain
and repetitious refrain.

LIVE AND LEARN

1981

I'm more concerned with pleasures
of the flesh
then with ramblings of the
mind.

You can still feel the pleasure
even though you may be blind
but a prisoner of the mind
is tied to his ways.
Whether they be self-chosen
or uniformly imposed,
the only way to freedom
is the road that grows.

Whether you take it
or leave it,
the river still flows.
Be the soldier of opportunity
and go to where he goes.

Blinded by the highway
that runs in the night,
walk the darkened hallway
to keep out of sight.

PIECES STILL GOOD

You can dig up graves
and smile from within.
You can take your medicine
but you can't forget your sin.

You can hide forever
from the things you fear,
but it don't mean
they'll ever disappear.

You can't run
from yourself.
There's nowhere to go.
It's all too clear,
so on with the show.

Seeing the shadows
and jumping with jitters,
it's only the night wind
and the unknown that glitters.
So go out socially
and pay the babysitters
but you know you're a phony
and you suffer for the quitters
and the marquee lights
keep on shining bright.

LIVE AND LEARN

12/2/81

> The final end
> has yet to be written
> and there's no reason
> to skip over the pages
> before us now!
> Let's live them.
>
> Quiet, silence
> hear the music
> in your soul…
> dance to it.
>
> Enjoy your sunrises
> and tea in the morning
> and enjoy the land
> laid before you…
>
> Sooner or later
> You'll face yourself
> and cry
> and then
> and only then
> will you really know why.

PIECES STILL GOOD

Shimmers of light
glimmers of hope
walk straight and free
avoid that hanging rope.

LIVE AND LEARN

12/25/80
(CHRISTMAS DAY)

Nobody knows, Mom.
Not many care
I wish too —
that you could make it all better.

Damn crazy
that's what I am.
Cruisin' down the river
on the West Side Highway.

City blowin' my mind
I turn around
go home —
could be paranoia.

No cause for alarm
joy is the call.
Holiday spirit
for one and all.

Twister strikes
but it only hits me.
Everyone walkin' round
in circles they can't see.

PIECES STILL GOOD

Feelin' things
that I'm sure others know
but the sorrow that it brings
only adds up to fruitless woe.
And what good's the woe
without the fruit?

Use this lesson
to benefit myself
I believe, she believes
I'll be happier without her —
do better,
be better.
It's amazing that I believe her
but I do.

I always thought I was the prophet
or I was the teacher
but I was wrong.
She is the educated one
in this instance.
I am merely the child.

LIVE AND LEARN

11/11/81

Do we have any capable minds out there at all?
Minds uncluttered by the full day's wind blowing in
my eye?

I must admit to being a bit confused in general
in reference to the general confusion all around me.
I think a drink would be appropriate. Furthermore
I think there are other things that are equally
appropriate yet unjust.

Is the Florida Express the plane that goes down in
the ocean, or does it merely fly graced by the Lord?
I won't drown in no ocean, and I am graced by
the Lord. Together that leaves me anywhere I choose
to be as the sun sets over Syracuse. Now there's a
big lie because we all know there is no sun in
Syracuse. So what do you think of that one?

PIECES STILL GOOD

No drinks and no free tickets to anywhere anymore, and there's no justice there, much less payment. What we have here is a severe lack of bucks, no buckaroos, bucko. Negator on the silver dollar of life, but everything else is coming up splendidly, everything from the purple mountains and gray skies I saw last night to the clear blue skies I hope to see tonight.

LIVE AND LEARN

1981

I don't mind
but it comes as quite a shock
when the story unwinds
and it speed up the clock.

All of a sudden
Everything's nothin'
you're lost in the mud
when you find yourself questioning
or trying to rationalize
any of this absurdity we call life.
We have no control, none whatsoever
over our ultimate destiny.

Everything we do,
anything we touch
is just momentary.

Our thoughts
our feelings
aren't owed to any.
They are just nightmares
in a snowstorm
dead batteries that will never start.

PIECES STILL GOOD

We know not the true cause
nor do we really care.
Unfortunately we are content
with what is given.
Screw it, I haven't said what I intended to say.

LIVE AND LEARN

12 / 2 / 81

> I feel the Lord's power
> streaking thru me like
> lightening.
>
> I never will sour
> on my eternal life's hike
> and never once find it frightening.

PIECES STILL GOOD

12/16/80
(CHRISTMAS TIME UPON US)

First of all, I was standing in Central Park today
Great scene today, many great scenes in recent times,
some much too intense, others just right.
You survive those boy,
and you got it made. Good Luck.

Sometimes —
I long for summertime;
moonlight rides —
sweat smell
like perfume.

Too much gloom
in wintertime —
nighttime —
come too soon
floats away like
some balloon.

Ballgames — swimming,
it gets depressing
to be left guessing.
Was he for real

LIVE AND LEARN

or just messing?
Thankfully I proceed
with his blessing.

Could it be, comrade?
It's all just crap.
Could be
I've had enough of that.

I'm a heartbroken buddy
but hey, that's nothing new.
I need something
to hold on to.
Hey…what about you?

PIECES STILL GOOD

12/2/81

Parade up and down the river,
parade up and down the street,
parade in your shoes,
parade in your feet.

Lead your band
and always sing your song
remember that —
to always sing your song.
When everything's all done
and finished,
no one will remember anyway.
So you might as well
have sung your own song!

Celebrate the land.
Celebrate the light.
Too much wrong in the land,
too much wrong in the night.

LIVE AND LEARN

1981

Windows — people's faces
brick walls, bare trees
forget your clothes, sonny,
you liable to freeze.
Call the doctor
if their baby sneeze.

It's a sick world, baby,
but I do love it.
Even the momentary
uncertainty of it all.
It's a gas.
Life's a ball.

Love them pieces —
make a choice
either you win or lose.

You know the game never ceases
as long as you hear the voice.
So why waste your time cryin' the blues?

Howdy-doody.

PIECES STILL GOOD

1981

You know boys
sometimes I'm astounded.
All these predicaments
are truly unfounded.

You may walk proud
Head held high down the street.
Seems like the old crowd
all stood on their feet.

No, nothing's changed
but who's to say that's bad?
If there's contentment
then so be it —
content.

The Lord lets us live
all he asks is we do such.
Are we soldiers of the universe?
Or warriors of the Lord?
Are we merely carpenters?
Here only to build?
And will we ourselves
reap the final reward?

LIVE AND LEARN

If there ain't no heaven
this must be hell.

Daddy blue,
space age materials,
toy rocket ships,
concord planes,
rolling planes,
model planes,
it's all very plain to see.

Eat it all.
Crap it out.
Find the formula.
Shout it out.

If this is prose
then anything goes
up my nose…
panty hose…
her teeth holding a rose…
None of this fulfills my woes.

Saw a purple sky
last night.
Picturesque-romantic,
haunting, wild —
all that from just
one sky,
Now there's a bargain for you.

PIECES STILL GOOD

7/1/80

Walkin' in your spirit
Feelin' your vibrations
as I get near it,
light up with new sensations.

It's insane the way
I used to be.
Now I'm together
with my spirit and me.

It's so easy to say yes
turn around and say no.
I'd gladly regress
if you could only see.

Man, I've found you
I feel it's true.
I believe in your power
no chance to misconstrue.

Fill me, Lord.
Will me, Lord.
I'll carry your sword,
never be bored.

LIVE AND LEARN

My friends are liars
they ain't going nowhere
for all my lovin'
I'd better beware.

It's a shame
people can't see.
They let me down.
I'll be laughin'
in my mansion.

Don't wanna
lend no dimes.
Baby, you will never
crucify me
for someone else's crimes.

Thanks for the lack
of confidence.
Reminds me of who I
really am.
I'm the lone soldier
and I gotta fight.
Pick my friends
better pick em right.
I'm riding high,
ALRIGHT!

PIECES STILL GOOD

11/23/80
(IT'S ALL OVER NOW, AND I AIN'T EVEN BABY BLUE)

    I'm so alone now
    as History repeats
    tear out my heart
    knock me to my feet

    Oh, baby
    I can't even cry
    you fly away
    cut that tie

    Everything I had
    given to you
    was I cruel, baby
    or just a fool

    Sure we'll stay friends
    but I ain't even stayin'
    It feels like the end
    and yes I've been prayin'

LIVE AND LEARN

prayin' you'd see the light
and remember my smile
prayin' we could get it right
and go on for a while

I worshipped
I'm crushed
I loved everything about you
but you turned me into slush

I can't express the sadness
seething from my vein
I can't express the madness
driving me insane

Oh darling,
this lonely heart's weepin'
it used to laugh with joy
when we talked of our little boy
but now hatred be creepin'
up through my heart

sideswiped, jacknifed
no I wasn't too smart

You won't listen
to a damn thing I'm saying
You figure for sure
you know best
God bless you, baby

PIECES STILL GOOD

I hope you're peaceful
now that you've laid me to rest

Like the Holy Ghost
I'll rise from the grave
if you be in trouble
I will come to you and save
but we through
but I love you

So go ahead
And do what you will
to whomever you do please
right now I'm dying
but put your handkerchief away I'm
not dead

I loved your brown eyes
I loved talkin' to you
You're makin' this so hard
I love you so much
I really do

You go find
Your perfect man
don't worry that you left me
drownin' when he's wining and
dining you and he takes to clownin'
and you smiling and laughing cause
you think you love him so

LIVE AND LEARN

Remember me —
then baby
after he's through with you
and he tells you that he's got to go!

You were my inspiration,
I needed you bad
You done me wrong
I never been so sad

Sure I'll hang on
salvage what I can
from this twisted wreck
but you shot me, baby
bullets flying everywhere
I'm hurt bad-lying there on the deck

I want you back
tell me it's a mistake
dry these tears
stop the tremor from this quake

Ah but, baby,
you're lost to the devil
you're drunk on his sperm
he's gonna mess you up bad, baby
and then crush you like a worm

and I'll take care of myself
from here on in
Vodka, Southern Comfort, O.J. and Sloe Gin

PIECES STILL GOOD

Oh, baby, I'll stand upon a mountain
and I'll be there all alone
can't talk to you
not even on the phone
you go, follow your attraction
you're the real side show
freaks knockin' on your door

I tried, baby
I loved, baby
You did too
(I know that)

It's over
and I'm cryin'
Don't stop me now
I'm building a river
damn the dam

LIVE AND LEARN

HOW NICE

      How nice was it?
      nice
      How nice was I?
      nice
      Whatever became of it?
      And who the hell is he?

      How did I kiss?
      nice
      How did I make love?
      nice
      Then what became of me!

PIECES STILL GOOD

7/11/80
TO DAD

> Forget them sounds
> that come from downtown.
> Forget rock and roll music
> that spins me around.
>
> Forget that folk
> sound like ostrich.
> Forget that reggae
> don't hold me hostage.
>
> Yeah, you take downtown
> take uptown too
> but I'll take Condon's
> when I'm feeling blue.
>
> Flowin' through
> like cocaine medicine,
> Condon's sweet jazz
> wipe away all the sin.
>
> Sooth my eyes,
> ease my mind,
> erase my fears,
> leave them behind.

LIVE AND LEARN

Let the boys
scream rock and roll.
Let the classics
take their toll.

Let the funk
rot with the disco.
You can have the punk…
to Condon's I'll go.

You can take the ladies,
you can take the applause.
I'll rock with the babies
to the Dixieland cause.

Stamp and shout
move your feet
say it with clout
to that Condon's beat.

Yeah Dixieland
Yeah Condon's
yeah my jazz playin' man
to the jazz heaven, I have been.

PIECES STILL GOOD

6/2/80

Miss my guitar
miss the summer in the ville
miss the days of riches
and the mountains by the hill.

True, I've had my fill,
but time stands not still.

Miss the blood
flowin' through my system.
Miss the juices
flowin' through my vein.
Miss the buzzards in the morning.
Lord, I miss the cocaine.

See the city
in my suit and tie
my days of leisure, gone.
They echo of my far away cry —

My youth sadly lost
in the days that seem best.
Lived them like a lion
and buried them to rest.

LIVE AND LEARN

It's nice to remember
the time and the smiles.
Come some time in November
I'm going back for a while.

Joy, pain
sufferin'
qualudes, bondage
and bufferin'

So many different
directions.
Huge categories
of selections.
Choose, brother
Lose, brother.

I'm floating away
I'm enjoying it though.
It's the price I pay,
didn't you know.

I give it all away
but I had my loves.
Someday I'll grab it to stay
or I'll join a fan club.

PIECES STILL GOOD

11/23/80

Why can't I save you
sister of my night?
Why do my piercing cries
go unanswered?

Why the fright
from within yourself
uncertainty your thermometer.

I'd give an eye
to have your heart
untouched and pure
from the start.

Don't look at me
and I won't look at you
and we can make-believe
we didn't conceive
of each other as lovers.

Listen, lover,
there was no other.
I sit dismayed
poison had been sprayed.

LIVE AND LEARN

I'm helpless to stop it
the truth is you really ain't worth it.
You're close,
but you really ain't worth it.
But it hurt like hell anyway.

I'm such a fool
such a stranger
but it's not what life does to you,
is it?
It's what you do to life.

Is there a resting place
for a murdered soul
or have you easily erased
everything about me that you know?

I'll get my justice
I swear that to you.
But then I won't be able to share it
even though I'd like to.

Sweetheart,
I love you,
but I'll be moving on.
So don't worry
bout' me hanging on.

But first I gotta get dressed!

PIECES STILL GOOD

11/23/80

You be with somebody else
and I'm sitting here with losers,
firecrackers exploding at my feet.

I've been a fool
and now I'm praying for grace.
I must look upwards now.

I'm talking to little kids
way below my level of play,
and I'm left holding the bag.
I'm the only one left to pay.

Oh, it hurts to be trampled
especially from behind.
Lord, give me the strength
to make up my mind.

Let me rise again
and never let down.
Let me live down
the lies I've lived.

LIVE AND LEARN

Forgive me, Lord,
I praise thee.
I need your strength
and security.
I need love
and your smile from above.

Lord, I need strength.
Please give it to me.
Lord, heed me
set me free
and I am yours.
There can no longer
be any other cause.

The sinners must be punished
one by one.
I must straighten out and organize
the man I know I am.

No champagne — no cocaine
just another sucker in
another jam.

I'm the sucker, man.
I need that ladder again.
Gotta start climbing.

PIECES STILL GOOD

11/23/80

All I know is
I'm just sitting here
while everyone's out
getting ahead…

I can't move
I'm frozen,
wasted meat
better off dead…

I need the inspiration
that comes from your heart,
but you lied to me, baby,
and I fell apart.

Must be constructive
I've destroyed enough already.
There's no need for fear
even if I'm not ready.

I'm hungering for contentment
but I'm caught up in emotion.
I need an old witch
to mix me just the right potion.

LIVE AND LEARN

Seems like I been down
this spiral staircase before.
Only this time
it's head first.

Can't quite condone
the action you took
and your timing
was certainly the worst.

Yeah, you a saint...
and Tattoo-he a giant...
and the sky
ain't the sky at all.
It's the sea turned upside down
and emptied on my face.

Goodnight, lady.
Goodnight, sir.
Isn't there anything I can do
that won't remind me of her?

Chemical warfare
kamikaze style.
Yeah, I know I wasn't born there
but I'll adapt, it'll only take a while.

Rampaging madness
my blood is burning
(smells like burnt blood)
my mind is churning.
But my heart — he is breaking with sadness.

PIECES STILL GOOD

1981

Sometimes being comfortable
ain't where it's at,
but it's nice to have a choice.

Got to get back to my roots
but they're buried deep beneath
the earth.
I loved my baby
but that got me nowhere,
for whatever it was worth.

There might be justice
or just bad timing.
Hard to distinguish the two.

But there's no malice
in my heart
even though I'd like to
take care of a few.

I just hope someday
I'm seeing clearly
and someday I'm riding tall.
Right now I'm suffocating

LIVE AND LEARN

hanging on dearly
feeling so small.

Come save my soul
I'll pay the toll
and then time can take me…
wherever it like.

Falling apart at the seams.
That's how it seems.
Star-spangled glitter.
frustration,
simulation,
ejaculation,
none of it magic elixir.

I've got all my own space,
but my mind has left me,
flown off in space,
left sorrow in its place.

Seems I've been fixing to do
some good things
the walls came a crumbling
and down went my dreams.

Oh crap,
is this destiny —
tragedy or reality
or a rainbow by the sea?

1981

Supposed to be somewhere.
I don't go.
Why?
I don't know.

Didn't eat
nothin'
hungry as a hog.
Everything's closed.

Take a trip
up and down
the road.

Couldn't decide
where to go
strange — actually
that I did not know
insane — factually
but hidden so.

Jeepers,
lend me your hand
pull me out of all this
quicksand.

LIVE AND LEARN

Save me
from this deserted land.
Must rise above the Christmas tree
sit on top.

PIECES STILL GOOD

12/2/81

I remember walking up
many covered steps
to an Olympus all my own,
and I remember being much younger then.

But I have bleached my soul
flushed it and replaced it
with "Lord's" guaranteed antifreeze.
Now I know I won't freeze
that doesn't mean I
won't burn in hell, in order
to escape that fate
you must believe in God's will
and live true!

But now I stand, eye to eye
as I reflect, towards myself.

He saved me from the
grizzliest of deaths
one of self-destruction!

Let honor be your guide
don't feel let down or low down
no matter how low you slide.

LIVE AND LEARN

Reach for his hand
let him pull you and lead you
through this deserted land.

PIECES STILL GOOD

4 / 2 / 81

>We don't have to
>talk about it
>positively-absolutely.
>
>No, I don't have to
>bring it up.
>You don't have to
>remember it.
>
>But don't you think
>that's really
>the easy way out?
>You always take the easy
>way out.
>
>Will you do it forever?
>Will you take the easy way
>forever, baby?
>
>Sweetheart,
>I call you that truly,
>like I don't know you,
>you don't know me.

LIVE AND LEARN

But we don't have to
talk about it,
we can bury it
keep it prisoner
never set it free.

At your request, baby,
any way you desire
you nearly drove me crazy
my needs screamed, so dire.

I'm recording the moment
right now,
that's what I'm doing.
Putting it down,
as I live it
responding to the
seconds allowances.

Consequential challenges,
that lay ahead for me
-the warrior,
a master of my trade
my tools solid and poised.

There are no fences
no obstacles
only a bright yellow pathway
enhanced by a
golden sunshine.

PIECES STILL GOOD

only a spark
ignites the hydrants
that sprinkle, forcefully
the sky
with colored
magical waters

on one hand
we have a perfect vision
an eternity of endless
joy
a lifetime of continual
satisfaction

fulfillment
expectation,
meditation,

and on the other hand
we have the same…

LIVE AND LEARN

1981

Walkin' in one direction
and one direction only.
Back to you
my subject matter
you matter.

You are so sweet
and blind.
You lost me,
you know that.

But I haven't lost
you no,
not as long as you're
still out there
floating around
free.

There's no way
you give up
without coming back
to me.
But I don't have to talk
about it
we'll just see.

PIECES STILL GOOD

Mechanical answers
repeated questions.
You and I, Black and White
the sun and moon
does one shine
while the other is dull?
Or do we simply
never see the others shining?

No, no more time
on you
certainly no more
rhyme on you

someday you'll read this
and maybe will laugh
but you'll love me then
and that's why you'll laugh
but you don't love me now
and that's why I'm laughing!

LIVE AND LEARN

12/2/81

>What it all boils down to
>Is what you have cooking in the pot!

PIECES STILL GOOD

1981

There's no tears,
The Lord can't wipe away

LIVE AND LEARN

5/12/81
(DAY OF THE RISING SOUL)

You had custody
of my heart
but you banished it
forever.

I'll never know
you again,
no never.

Sometimes I'll be
thinking 'bout you.
Most of the time
I remember you as cruel.

But it really
is my fault
if I choose to
be a fool.

Mystified
crucified
burned inside
taken for a ride.

PIECES STILL GOOD

all true
all true
all done
all done

Need me
Need you

Why waste time
never wasted
again?
The last time I saw you
I wondered who
I was makin' love to.
It's a shame
I remember you
that way.

Do the best I can
forever
for those
who love me.

Will never call you again,
no never.

You laid it
on the line
now you
walk it.

LIVE AND LEARN

6/17/77
CALIFORNIA –PHASE II

Beauty all around
in so many colors
looks real nice

surrounded by lovelies
bare-backed lovelies
fine as could be

watching the sunshine
fall all around
tan, tan, tan, and then brown

So foxy, looks so good
you know I would
I would

Waves rolling in at me
the sky hanging tight
the American flag waving in the air
boats assail at sea
and the fattest lady in the world
is showing her ass to me

PIECES STILL GOOD

Could be I'm dizzy
from all of this sun
buildings all behind me
I got no place to run

Nothing is everything
and everything is nothing
Bugs are eating me

Could be stoned
but that's over now
I'm looking at a honey
Oh wow, Oh wow

She's giving me eyeballs
I've seen before
glancing at me
looking for more
she got me going
and my heart's on fire
She's rich and creamy
and getting tan
I think I've seen
all I can stand
bug running down my ass
ain't bothering me
that fat lady's ass
is all I can see

LIVE AND LEARN

Two German ladies talking
one foxy for sure
love those German girls
hungry for more

Three babies crying loudly
an eagle soars ahead
three men of tomorrow
they better off dead

Hey, I'm just a rambler
but you know that already
living like a gambler
life ain't so steady

And I see the sunshine
and the sunshine see me
now how come you tell me
that you ain't free

Hey, I'm ramblin' now
rambling away
ramble right through
another day

The boardwalk beside me
and the sand underneath
the sky above
and the air all around
millions of places

PIECES STILL GOOD

wide open spaces
and millions of hideaway towns

Everybody hides
in their own town.
They remember that
when they travel around.
No place to go to
but another town
and that's no place to go.
I long for the people
in a faraway place
who live the best they know.

Content with the good times
and happiness
don't look for those highway signs.
They live in freedom
although they're trapped
and I lived trapped
although I'm free.
It's plain enough to see.

Now the sun is directly overhead
and I can't see it looking around.
Seems like everywhere I go
there's a new part of me I've found.

There's more to me
than meets the eye
and more to anybody

LIVE AND LEARN

than meets me.
But I don't care.
Guru lady with sunglasses
walks with hunchbacked kid
very weird.

I'll dig it one more time
and then I think I'll call it a day.
It doesn't even seem like
I really went away.

But I'll be back tomorrow
and yes, the sun will shine
and everything I feel here
at least I'm sure it's mine.

And so I float back
into the world at large
just looked at a map
and it is very large.

Before I go
I thought you might like to know
that my thoughts are going to pass
for once again in my face
I see that fat lady's ass!

PIECES STILL GOOD

6/14/77

CALIFORNIA- PHASE I

Sitting here with memories
by my side
I miss everybody
it's so easy to cry.

I long for the old times
with smiling faces
back in the old town
so many new places.

I'm out here sitting all alone
3,000 miles from my home.
I got women on my mind
seen too many highway sign.

Yes, I'm sitting in sorrow
trying to smile
I know I'll be going back
in a while.

I see the ocean
looking at me
I see the sky
hanging over the sea.

LIVE AND LEARN

And I see the people
lyin' all around
and somehow I wish
I was outta this town.

Too much confusion
and I'm drifting away
Total seclusion
it's the price I pay.

Hey, I got what I wanted
and I really am here
iced off forever
no one is near.

What am I really doing
too much of nothing
it's me I'm screwin'.
Keeping my head together
as best I can
comes a time in a man's life
and so I ran.

I been running forever
but never again
I've seen that all this running
just leads quicker to the end.

PIECES STILL GOOD

Hey I'm tired of fighting
the things in my past
I miss my memories
why couldn't they last?

Well what can I tell you
my friend back home.
Some men they work forever
and some they roam.

What's it really like?
I hear you asking me.
I try to explain,
I hope you can see.

Everybody sees himself
and nobody else
I miss the good times
I'm sorry I put them on the shelf.

Hey I'm straight as an arrow
and I thought I was shooting high
but now I'm here
all I got is the sky.

It doesn't really matter
I'll be back soon
but I'm the only one who knows
what it's like to live on the moon.

LIVE AND LEARN

Yea, things will get back together
and I'll fit right back in
but I'm the only one
who knows where I been.

Hey, I've seen the inner shadow
of the being I call me.
Yes, been to the end of my mind
I did not believe what I see.

I saw frustration
growing inside of me,
I saw determination
sitting leisurely.

I saw the frying pan
and on it was my brain.
I see the people now
they all look the same.

It's time to strike back
and do it up.
Too much confusion
I blew it up.

Now I'm satisfied
cause I've seen the end,
and now I long
for a friend.

PIECES STILL GOOD

Well I'm happy inside
but I'm crying again.
I know I went for a ride
but I did not bend.

And now I understand
what makes a man.
It's the right to be happy
any way you can.

So soon I'll be there
just like I never left.
I'll be telling them stories
that will sound like the best.

Yeah, I'll be all together
like everyone else,
but nobody's been through
all of himself.

Why did I do it?
I can't explain
but now I've found the breaking point
of my pain.

Yeah, I will hang out
and stick it through.
I'll follow this journey
and then I'll follow you.

LIVE AND LEARN

Hey, I'm free as a bird
but I can't say a word
nobody's listening
cause nobody heard.

PIECES STILL GOOD

12/20/80

Now listen to me
my friend
things are mellow
certainly you miss her
long for her
desire burning inside…
but you're strung up
and out
and destiny calls…
it might take you nowhere
it might be your loss
or maybe you make it, son,
if you choose the right course

Yes, you ache for her smile
your cry for her heart
but there's something inside of her, boy,
that pulled you apart

Captain, you're in charge
so sail this ship to port
make the game plan
go for the kill
and don't get caught

LIVE AND LEARN

Brenda, Brenda, you're not being fair
open my heart
and let me close enough to share
you mind find a different lover
but does he really care
no time for lectures
no time to beware
you're my heart throb, baby
but I'm coming up for air

I'm walkin' in my boots
listening to my footsteps
fearful, for once
...of the silence

I can't comprehend
this newfound trend
that takes my baby's love
and substitutes violence
today was not the greatest
of days
but I made it through
clearly a good sign

I look forward to rising tomorrow
early and happily
Let my true love await
I'm not afraid anymore

I'm not worried about losing it
It's gone already...

PIECES STILL GOOD

I have to try to get it back
if I want it back
I can design a plan
A time plan, a formula
might be intense

I can't wait to get up early tomorrow
and conquer the world
Bob Wilbur, Eddie Condon
Rick Sands and of course,
Jorge Rouque

It's coming back to me
recollections of the prophet
crystal clear
like stream water

Can't play games
and put up with people's innuendos
my fate never
ceases to amaze me
it's truly a gift
thanks

Mustn't stop now
it's a good time to press on (thanks, Bobby)
yes, onwards and upwards
I'm leaving something behind
and that hurts
and there's fear, a little fear
that I might never find it (her) again

LIVE AND LEARN

But I really got no choice
I must keep movin'
and who knows
I just might find a new friend

So I'm excited
for the prospects are many
and although I haven't been invited
I'm coming through that wall
bustin' through that wall
try and stop me
Enemies of the past
they all must fall
each and everyone
one and all

The dreaded path
the losers take
the question marks
in friends lives

Hey Superman
can you see through my heart
wish you luck, honey,
happiness and joy
I've told you that already
why weren't you listenin'

PIECES STILL GOOD

"Yes, there's a fool feelin' lonely (Tall Dogs)
and he looks a lot like me."
Hi, Earl
Not Earl's red pants
not Earl Tall Dogs

Red, White and Blue
I love you
even though
you told me not to

don't say it, darlin'
don't say we're through
you must be mistaken
it's coincidence
ain't no clue
I love you,
I love you

LIVE AND LEARN

12/2/81

Astrologers assemble
for the charade of the stars
call together all members of the assembly
and give them lifelong scars.

Scold them, like they burned us
brand them with silencers.
Don't want to hear no fuss.

In the long run
the dilemmas we face
here on earth
are not very significant.
As a matter of fact
they're ever less significant now,
but I realize that's impossible
for you (and me) to see.

PIECES STILL GOOD

3/15/81

Who may I say?
May I say?
What's on my mind
I'd like you to know
that sometimes
when I'm feelin
blue
I'd like to get up and go
seems like
that be the case
most of the time
walk the line
pay the fine
decipher
your own deception
and the boundaries
it inflicts

the precious
influence
can be detected
but it still gets no respect
the skyline
fall down

LIVE AND LEARN

go away
don't need you anymore

Goodbye, moonbeams,
enjoy the ride
Cut those cards
open the door
let the air in
air out

PIECES STILL GOOD

12/2/81

>Don't put no flowers on my grave
>save your money and have lunch on me!

LIVE AND LEARN

3/12/81
COME AND GET IT

When you need
my love,
come and get it.

You don't heed
my love,
but you'll regret it.

I won't be
your love
no, you won't let it.
When you need my love,
come and get it.
I can see your
love,
but I can't get it.

I'm not free
from your love,
so I can't forget it.

When you need my love,
come and get it.

PIECES STILL GOOD

Might be a mistake,
child —
inept characterization.

You might have taken
me for a while,
sincere misrepresentation.

Or you could have
bowed to Buddha
in tribute to a nation.

But you stayed
at home
and faced up to the
situation.

Now you're dead
and gone
and my heart is breakin'.
When you need my love,
come and get it.
You can be my love.
Yes, I'd let it.

LIVE AND LEARN

1981

Imitations
of present sensations
get nowhere

Your true expression
of deep confession
and nobody could care

Endurance of absurdity
accomplished nothing...
no change in sight

Quality
replaced by speed
stand and watch it happen

Cryin' hunger
true need
stand around laughin'

Bank vaults
insurance with no faults
violence among the poor

PIECES STILL GOOD

Crying babies
indefinite maybes
nobody cares

Insecurity
rages through the flesh
hidden by bravado
crushed by death

Personalities
celebrities
idolized as gods

Politicians
and religion
viewed as senseless fog

Endless highways
point up to the sky
but cannot yet reach so high
Babies unborn
umbilicals untorn
welcome to the world of scorn

LIVE AND LEARN

12/2/81

>Crimestoppers
>can't stop you
>busses pass you
>by
>at bus stops
>you can fly over
>rooftops
>but you can't steal
>my heart
>
>From the treetops
>you can see me
>you can grab me
>but you can't keep
>me down forever.

PIECES STILL GOOD

1981

Destiny —
merely the measure of success
To take hold of your own
means taking blame
for the mess
to be forcibly thrown
means weakness you confess
they call it a choice,
but it's really a guess

They offer courage
by bestowing
an all knowing reassurance
claiming that you've been blessed
but you realize you dreamin'
so wake up and get dressed
walk out that door
the road to success

LIVE AND LEARN

1981

>   We see the signature of our souls
>   reflected in the actions of our lives.

PIECES STILL GOOD

12/2/81

> I want an airplane full of money
> to crash land thru my window
> everything else I already have!

LIVE AND LEARN

1981

> Why does it seem
> like a Cadillac dream
> with yesterday's misfortunes
> as its engine?
>
> What does it mean
> to speak of a dream
> and brave the obstacles
> no matter the pain?
>
> Can't it be so
> that even though
> the years come and go
> there's something beside
> just foolish pride
> that paves the golden floors
> through which I go?
>
> Can't it be true?

PIECES STILL GOOD

5 / 19 / 81

I always thought I was the lucky one.
I never realized it was the Lord's guiding hand.

LIVE AND LEARN

12/5/80

Down by the reservoir
I sit stoned silent
looking at my brand new car.
I'm feeling violent.

Down by the sea
water pushing and shovin'
workin' so hard
to get itself up on me.

Up in the mountain
together with the sky
I sit there countin'
all the reasons why.

I'm over in the farm fields
blue jeans on
thinking up new crops
to grow on the farm.

Out there in outer space
I float so peaceful
finally found my own place
people can be so deceitful.
It don't pay anymore
to save face

saying grace is good.

PIECES STILL GOOD

1981

How do you define
the most precise of drawn
line
that split the beings
you and I?

I've learned to
see straight
through
the diamonds when
they shine.
I've been converted
to a brother
the choice is solely mine.

I understand the
spectrum
of the sky.

The occupational hazards
of life
and being caught
without a tie.

LIVE AND LEARN

Señor,
siesta master,
you with the smile
on your face,

You stare at
me
so happily
bring sunshine
smiles,
to my face
make it a better
place.

Sinister faces
may pass you
but you remain
high, aloft
atop the solid foundation
you've laid.
You are rested
uncontested
and among the
very best of men.

You are thoughtful,
wise,
you offer no disguise.

You do not
misquote

PIECES STILL GOOD

and you are not
misquoted.
Your deeds,
magnificent,
rarely unnoticed.

Caring concern
and the power that burn
with the feeling to learn
the plan and the turn.

You are my brother
closer than any
a salute (twenty-one guns at least)
my tribute.

Yes, friend,
the warmth
is among us
grazing and glazing
with its warmth
the only way
to go.

You are my teacher
My friend
My brother
My companion
My mother
My father.
I love you.

LIVE AND LEARN

3/13/81
TELL IT LIKE IT IS

    I don't need
    to talk to nobody.
    I trust myself.

    I've overcome
    and been overcome by
    many things I've tried to
    apply discipline to.

    Nobody dictates to me
    cause I wouldn't listen…
    I'd get up and
    walk away.

    Nobody mistreats me
    and yes I've risen
    above the promises you
    throw my way.

    But I leaped like
    a frog
    upon your kitchen floor.
    you said, " get outta here,
    you dog,
    you ain't no puppy anymore."

PIECES STILL GOOD

3/31/77

Plato, Socrates and all of the boys
played all their lives with philosophical toys.
I wonder how they ever stood the noise.

I wonder if they retained their poise.

They argued about life and everything else.
They called it justice, the search for the self
and The Republic lies dormant on my shelf.
I'd like to inquire as to their wealth.

But they definitely were cool
because they could spot the fool
and show him he was mistaken
from so much thinkin',
a brain could be awakin'.

They saw life as it was to be seen
with perception the sharpest, and insight so keen.
They sought to bleed for the truth
no lies — that would be uncouth.

They sought the key to life and to the planet
perhaps they slightly over ran it.

LIVE AND LEARN

But nevertheless they were on the right track
I only wish I could bring them back.

They knew they were living
and insisted upon giving.
They shared their knowledge of the world
and into outer space their heads were hurled.

In a society blinded by reality
where prisoners of the minds thought they were free,
a man called Socrates claimed to be their guide.
Yet they would not accept him — too much pride.

Now generations come and go
and people yearn to know.
They claim they seek the almighty light…
the light nobody sees, but it burns so bright.

Ah, yes, they say, Socrates was correct,
yet his ways they still neglect.
For they are no better than their fathers
the wisdom is there, yet no one bothers.

The people who see it
know it for sure
for those who don't
there can be no cure.
Socrates knew it, Plato too…
of men like this there are very few.

PIECES STILL GOOD

Nevertheless the world exists,
yet Socrates does not
And the truth remains, it cannot be forgot.
So use the past and learn from Socrates mistakes.
Live with justice, that's all it takes.
You got to make your own breaks,
only you decide if they is real or fakes.
Still you also get to decide about me
I rest on a bed of security.
For all I know I see,
and I am truly free.
I have known it all along
through all the different me's
now I've seen the result.
Thank you, Socrates.

LIVE AND LEARN

3 / 29 / 77

I was one with everyone at one time
I felt like everything I saw was mine
I didn't want to leave anything behind
excuse me, hope you don't mind

I see the night, all 12 hours
I'm awake all the while, I use my powers
So go plant some flowers
will call them ours

I'm counting the minutes
and they're going pretty quick
I'm waiting for the finish
I think it's a pretty good trick

Everybody's going crazy
everybody includin' me
yeah, everybody going crazy
'cept no one can see

Everybody is a junkie
and you get to actin' like a monkey
when you going for another fix
you get to see people use all their best tricks

PIECES STILL GOOD

Sometimes things happen so fast
and sometimes it seems like nothing will last
sometimes it goes so easy
and sometimes everybody gets so damned sleazy
and it sure is freezing
and it ain't too pleasing
to see you sneezing
in my handkerchief
take out my guitar, play a riff

Everybody going insane
everybody is feeling the pain
none are exempt
some do attempt
to get free
no one's moving forward
they're all crazy

The man here, he does his mescaline
I look at him
another man calls it LSD
I used to call it THC
now it calls me

Yet I say I may be going too
then I look around, just see cows screamin' "moo"
Yeah, Hee Haw animals, eat the zookeepers' feed
some call it religion — I call it greed

Yet everybody's fryin' the same source
looking for their minds and bodies to divorce

LIVE AND LEARN

and sometimes, we all must meet the force
the winners, come out the boss
no one can stand the loss
sometimes it's decided by a toss
everyone plays, of course

Yeah, and everybody seems to be burning the light
watching the sunsets, cursing midnight
somewhere along the line they may lose their sight
everything becomes bright
love becomes fright
and wrong becomes right

Everybody sees themselves
although they don't see nobody else
and it doesn't matter that there is no sense
life is lived by the seconds, filled with suspense
the pleasure is intense
the weight, immense

Now I sit and wonder about it
the pieces just now beginning to fit
What can all this possibly mean
Everybody's tippin over —
don't know which way to lean

PIECES STILL GOOD

11/27/80

I'd like to give you something
that explains how I feel,
but words couldn't do that.

Just know that I am yours forever
be it body
or soul.

Just know
I view you as heaven
whose heart must
be nourished to grow.

Just know
I understand
as much as my
mind permits.

Always know
that I love you
regardless
of where
this little guy sits.

LIVE AND LEARN

Just know that
I want you
and yes,
those are my screams.

Just know
that we are
never apart
and yes,
those are my dreams.

Just hoping
that you knock
on my door again.
I feel richer but sad.
Yes, that's how it seems.

Just know
you're wanted
no matter where you be.
You'll always be right by my side
And yes those are my dreams.

PIECES STILL GOOD

12/2/81

Let the testimony begin
let the witnesses proceed
the proceedings begin
and the beginnings get started.

Let's hang 'em already,
why wait?
because we are a democracy
of fools —
is that why?

Let the judge judge
and the jury decide
to strip a man naked
and then steal his pride.

Let's condemn him for life
that bastard son
he must've done the bad deed
or he wouldn't have run.

LIVE AND LEARN

Who are we to decide
the fate of another
be he a lover, a sinner,
a father or a brother
Look yourself in the mirror judge
are you still ready to testify?

PIECES STILL GOOD

3/30/77

Big days ahead
as I lie in bed
thinking of what's been said
Big days ahead

Good times not far
as I dream of my sports car
covered you in tar
Good times not far

Sun will shine
as I walk the line
just biding my time
Sun will shine

Morning is near
so I should not fear
I have no fear
Morning is near

Heavy trips gone by
been pretty high
the brain did fry
heavy trips gone by

LIVE AND LEARN

Good loves, there were many
didn't cost me a penny
didn't marry any
Good loves, there were many

The future is now
So I'll take a bow
it matters, somehow
the future is now

The present has arrived
I have survived
It's time to sleep
I hear the beep

Goodnight to my dreams
it surely seems
to be the best means
to get through this night
Goodnight my dreams
sleep tight

PIECES STILL GOOD

1978

Boots are off
and the world is asleep
I'm awake, having a good time
a real fine time

Gonna have a better time tomorrow
doing it up
no false sorrow
do it up

Pity is a sin
to those who get it
so why pity?
Why write?
Why buzz?
The buzz is great
buzz, buzz, buzz.
Yeah, buzz.

LIVE AND LEARN

1977

After hours and all night long
I sit around and sing my song.

All the people, they come and go
some are crazy.
Others know.

Cannot write
once again
seems I must
drop my pen.

Say goodnight
with a smile
do some cocaine
in a while.

PIECES STILL GOOD

2/25/77 (6.30 A.M.)

Yeah high flying on a cocaine train
enjoying the ride
high flying and singing loud
never gonna slide

Just did it up
did it up right
feels so good
in the middle of the night

brain so fine
and everything mellow
another time
gums like Jell-O.

Good cocaine
enough to sustain
even the darkest rain
don't feel no pain.

Way to go,
Eskimo.

LIVE AND LEARN

2/27/77
(END OF THE COKE,
JOHNNY GOES HOME)

My good friends
are up and gone
going on back
to their farm
easy boys, nice and slow.
Can't afford any tickets, you know.

You showed me good times
while you stayed.
It sure was great
seein' you again.

You left my life
and way back then
I wondered when
I'd see you again.

True to your word
you remained my friend
I will never forget that
in the end.

PIECES STILL GOOD

You did me good
and I knew you would
for a friendship
has been built.

Now if I know one million men,
most I'll never see again
for friendships
some do wilt.

But you were cool
and you showed your faith
you proved yourself
it was worth the wait.

You write your songs
to the people in the past
cause you want those memories
to last and last.

You cling to everyone you can
as you quickly break away
and I never knew another man
who would rather stay.

So you left us behind
to smoke our dope
good things I hope you find.
I hope, I hope.

LIVE AND LEARN

You brought your friend
a legend was he.
Good vibes he did send
and now he's a friend to me.

You knew me since I was very young
and you sort of watched me grow.
I was sure my father's son
yet my brother you did know.

You showed me truth
in a world of lies.
I still can see it
when I look into your eyes.

You set examples
I watched you move.
You gave out samples
on these I grooved.

Still I've known you
in a light
that is straight and true
with no lack of sight.

You were my brother
when I needed a brother.
You were my friend
when I needed a friend.
You have given me friendship
that will not bend.

PIECES STILL GOOD

So go back home,
my cocaine friend,
and then go roam
that California trend.
See the sites
make the best partyin' nights
get plenty of rest.

Enjoy the good times
that you have.
Thanks for the good times
that we had.

The wind flies
and so do you
howlin' all night,
"I'm coming through."

You make it, bro,
this I can surely say.
You can earn every single goal
you already high flyin'
on your way.

LIVE AND LEARN

1981

>The greatest electrical charge can be obtained
>when the creative plug enters the creative socket,
>at the same moment the heart is broken!
>
>Even the greatest of barge can be pushed aside in
>a "coup d'etat"
>even the plushest of a rug
>an owner sometimes must hock it,
>when he is broke and choking!

PIECES STILL GOOD

3 / 4 / / 7 7
(JOHNNY RETURNS)

4 a.m. is a sleepy time
for a couple of friends of mine

Asks me questions
I don't want to answer
tells me things
I don't want to hear

Trouble ahead, trouble behind
trouble everywhere I go
tolls to pay
and some more trouble, you know

Nothing like before
and finally I see
that it doesn't really matter at all

For times past
and times ahead
they are parties in my head

Partying away every day
too much partying I say
can't always have things my very own way

LIVE AND LEARN

Tired and riding an all-night buzz
and there ain't no reason
just because

Hey, kid, you rode right to the top
kept on trucking and you would not stop
then you looked over that mountain top
and saw nothing at all
It was wasted time
yes, just wasted time
you tried to sing it in rhyme
but all it was
was wasted time

 Inequalities
and nobody sees
what's going down
drugged out campus
of tragedies
but nobody looks around
Good night my friend
sleep very well
it don't matter now
and it never will

PIECES STILL GOOD

10/14/81

If working is so wonderful, strengthening and mind building. And if that "lazy, lousy, do nothing life" my parents cautioned me to avoid, is really so lousy, then why does everyone work so hard and consider just such a life (lazy, do nothing) as the payoff for working hard. If that kind of life is the payoff, then it's worth having now.

LIVE AND LEARN

GREAT TV QUOTES

"The world is not ruled by chance,
the devil can only win
if we play his game."
Mr. Roarke of Fantasy Island

"Love = Empty yourself and yet be filled."
Caine of Kung Fu

"Charity is learning to forgive others.
Wisdom is learning to forgive yourself."
Detective Kojak of Kojak

PIECES STILL GOOD

2/27/77

Hey good to see you, buddies,
you look the same to me.
Do I look the same to you?
I guess I do.

Hey everyone's different.
We've all been down the same road
except we don't know it.
Even I at times refuse
to believe someone could have the same feelings
as me,
but basically,
people who are on the same mental plane
take the same
mental trips.

So I'm right there with you, my friends,
seeing my mind right through to its ends.
Don't worry 'bout makin' amends.
Just carry with you the love I send.

I've said farewell to all of you before.
I ain't gonna say it anymore.
No reason to, it's not goodbye.
Yet we all must strive forward, and give it a try.
So if perhaps I tell you a lie,
it's only because I don t want you to cry.

LIVE AND LEARN

2 / 1 / 77

Men work as machines
doing jobs or whatever seems
to come up in the course of time
anything, there's something for everyone
anyone can be a bum
it's cheap

Secretaries eat blueberries
as men lust for their cherries
me — I lust too
although not necessarily for you
there's something I got to do
and that's live

If I knew everything,
and could predict the future
there'd be no reason
to live it out
Would there?

Going away would not change a thing
riches and fortune it would not bring
perhaps a view from the outside
perhaps a new course to ride
the answers lay not outside

PIECES STILL GOOD

but from within
since when do the world's characters
tell me where I've been?

Only a mind journey,
no need to hire an attorney
the defense rests
the mind is a trickster
sometimes it jests
nevertheless
one must not be overcome
by the burning sensation, screaming run
there is no way outside
of nothing.

LIVE AND LEARN

2 / 7 / 78

Jamesville Gang
they're a tough bunch of men
hard tastin' beers
hard tastin' women
then hard tastin' beers again.

Jamesville Gang
they're openly proud
shoot their bullets nice and loud.
Load, and reload
fire some more
fall, and crash
man dead on the floor.
Jamesville Gang
done killed four more.

Jamesville Gang
after a man
ran away with the wife of Big Dan.

Won't be running long in Oklahoma town
Big Dan and the gang gonna gun him down.
Jamesville Gang, don't hang around.
Jamesville Gang, don't make a sound.

PIECES STILL GOOD

There was a lawman named Gus,
who had a boy named Russ,
who was sheriff in a town called Clay.
Jamesville Gang they rob the bank
they blew that sheriff away.

Boy named Russ grew to be a man.
Jamesville Gang he could not stand
except there was no more Jamesville Gang
for their final gunshot had rang
and now just six old men remain.
Six old men with the Jamesville name.

Six old men now layin' dead
Jamesville Gang their tombstones read.
Sherriff Russ he let it go to his head
and now there lies a seventh man dead.

Jamesville Gang done and gone
the legend lives on down on an Oklahoma farm
where a new sheriff sits fearing no harm.
After every storm, there comes a calm.

LIVE AND LEARN

1978

I'm not partyin'
and there's lots of snow.

Tryin' to cheer up
hate to bum out
ain't drinkin' from no loving cup
can't even shout.

One thing for sure
it's hell to know the truth.
Bless the ones who simply
are content to live their lives.
Bless the ones who do not question
the wickedness of their own minds.
They are the ones who live
but they are also the ones who die.

I live too
except I live all the time
every minute,
every second,
never a rest.
I'm grateful for the chance
for in order to be, really be
you have to live, really live.

PIECES STILL GOOD

It's hard though,
really hard.
Sometimes too hard.
But it's okay.
I'm there.

I know I can make it
above all
I know I will make it

Dylan made it
I'll make it too and I will make it
and when I do
I'll know it
nothing will change
I know that
for even Dylan remains the same
tortured
yet it is the only way to live

Yet sometimes it's so hard
really hard

LIVE AND LEARN

12/1/81

I'm trying to see this
from your side
so I don't feel
my hurt.

Crushed me like a feather
while your tears flow
but I'll get better.
Lord, he know.

Did not deserve
to be unnerved
from the seat of my pants
not by your sweetness
or our romance.

So every now and then
when you're lonesome for a friend,
remember me.
For you I'd bend
until my end
but you hung me
with no jury,
and no judge can forgive
you for that —
especially not this one.

PIECES STILL GOOD

11/13/81

No explanation
for the terror in my heart
great expectation
failed to start
something, somewhere
pulled, me apart
I'm sitting here wasted
dodging the poison darts

But that's not all of it
the dead are dead
nothing that can hit
can hurt worse then what you said

but only I know that
only me
as a matter of fact
I believe I can see

There's depiction
straight forward
there's description
moving toward me
full forced, propelled
aimed at my eyes
I've listened to enough Bobby,
heard too many other lies

LIVE AND LEARN

There's Samsonite furniture
and jelly-like fish
neither budges
love smudges, your heart

Doctor Jimmy can't help me now
neither can Billy from planet Zyllis
and nobody yesterday
when I was hungry

but then I ate
and I was full

Time is a drifting
and I'm stuck between the hours
moving kinda slowly
I've lost all my powers

I'm just a paperweight
sitting on a desk
and you're just the paper
sitting underneath me
very messed up verse

PIECES STILL GOOD

12 / 1 / 81

It's still light out
but not for long
soon the sky'll turn black
crazy sky.
But don't feel left out —
seen the blackness of
the day.

Don't feel blacked out —
seen the wrongness
of my way.

Jumpin' around
like some clown
falling down
spinning around
everyone laughing all
around me.

Laugh fools.
Down by the River
I'll clean my soul
up on the spaceship
no one will know.

LIVE AND LEARN

12/2/81

Having weathered another rainstorm
but awaiting a brutal winter
and watching the dog (the pup)
romping (sleeping) on the floor.

I know what I must do
and I will do my best to do it —
from here on in
and from there on when.

Should I signal distress
I've paid for enough security
to pull me thru with success.

I can stand firm now…
even I'm amazed at my strength.
Yet fully understanding the ways of the world
workings of the mind
and spirit, holiness and loyalty
and especially the resurfacing of the Lord.

I see with clarity
the desperation ahead.
It bothers me to no end,
but it also leads to

PIECES STILL GOOD

the end I desire
and I will pursue it, at my choice
to any end!

Bored again
I could snore again
feeling sick as a dog

Need to get going
need energy flowing
I feel like resting in the morgue

Highways traveled
I've been there already
don't need no more

Just looking ahead
but instead
I see nothing in store
Oh well, dissipation blues
will just have to dissipate
and tomorrow's dreams
will just have to wait

Nothing doing
and no one around
living alone again
in this old town

Taking care of responsibility
bored to death

LIVE AND LEARN

wondering endlessly
holding my breath

Could be tomorrow
I'll sing a new song
Could be today
if I'm wrong

Normal again
and it's been a while
looking for a friend
and that down home smile

PIECES STILL GOOD

7/28/77

Yesterday I was a man,
today I don't know who I am.
Yesterday I was real,
today I don't know what I am.

Yesterday I was alive,
today I don't know if I can survive.

I'm on the ground
face all bloody
but I swear I ain't bleedin'.

I've been knocked down
but I'm standing up
got too many tickets for speedin'.

I was so up
now I'm so down
it's time I grow up
and slow down.

Tomorrow's still ahead
but I don't even see
down the path I've been led.
But that ain't really me.

LIVE AND LEARN

Tomorrow's coming soon
and right now it can't help me.
I can't even help myself
they gave me too much rope
and I finally hung myself.
My head belongs up there
on the "dead as ice" shelf.

Sure I'm sick
but I ain't got no temperature.
Everybody's sick
but nobody got no cure.

I can't believe this dark side of me
eating out my brain
lived long enough
to know this pain.

Now I'm crying
but I'm prayin' too
that someday
I'll find you.

Find me, will you?
And save my soul
I don't think I can do it
I'm too deep in the hole.

Got to climb out
but I can't move my legs

PIECES STILL GOOD

time to turn about
but I still have to beg.

Lend me your hand
and pull
I cannot stand
my mind is too full.

Save the glory
for my dying day.
Save the story.
There's gotta be another way.

Now I'm begging
and I'm trying hard
looking for the justice
but there ain't no justice
or maybe there is.

I'm so down in the ground
when I look around
I don't hear a sound
could it be that all I've found
is myself.

LIVE AND LEARN

Hell, it hurts bad
more than I can take.
I'm killing myself.
I'm about to break.

I'm killing everyone else too
and they don't deserve it.
I need a sunrise, a swim
and a new set of nerves.

PIECES STILL GOOD

1981

I want you now
so bad
Yes I do
but let me learn
from this, let me learn
nobody need compare
I need not compare
that wouldn't be fair

But I'm sadly
remembering you
and the wonderful things
that you did do
I need you
I need you

But I alone
must go on
with everything else
I got left to hold on to

I'd trade anything
if I could have you
but I can't
can't I convince you

LIVE AND LEARN

that we shouldn't wait
that being apart from you
ain't my fate

Please let me love you
I'm down on my knees
I'd do anything I have to
please, please

But no answer
lies in the wind
no dancer dances
the dance floor does rescind

And remember this, my friend
all the things you thought you wanted
don't mean anything
once you had them

But you
are you the same?
Why do you haunt me?
Why don't I hear you callin' my name?

There's so much irony
but so little love
it's only you
that I be thinking of
that's right, I miss you
I need you
so how's that for a laugh

PIECES STILL GOOD

nobody's laughing, nobody's cryin',
nobody's doing anything

LIVE AND LEARN

12/2/81

>Bootleggers
>run for their lives
>and I walk thru
>mine
>
>Down and out beggars
>with homemade, hidden knives
>waiting to pounce on you
>and you think everything's fine

PIECES STILL GOOD

2 / 6 / 81

> He who hesitates
> simply does not know!

LIVE AND LEARN

5/19/81

The Lord lets me forgive
but I'll never forget!

PIECES STILL GOOD

11/16/81

Do you know that it's time
when the friends start to leave?

Or is it time
when you start to bleed?

Do you think that it's time
when you heart starts to beat?
Or maybe it's time
when no shoes are on your feet.

Perhaps it's your time
when the moon she runs full.
Or maybe it's time
when the wagon start to pull.

Drag you along
claim for the better,
makes me madder and madder
don't say a word
don't want to upset her.

Down in the dumps
but this time not alone
never alone again,
caught in the slumps.

LIVE AND LEARN

No one is home
ain't my fault you were not home, brother,
never will be my fault
cannot be my fault.
Who told you to leave anyway?

Jesus, do you hear me
screamin' out your name?
Bleedin' on the street
crying out in pain.

This ain't the first time
I've been left behind
'cept this time I must keep moving
down the road with the white line.

You know I must keep moving.

You love me like a son
showed me I'm the one.
All that time
and all this while
takes an artificial pill
to make me smile.
Not for long
I'll break that record
forget that song
go in for the help
I need.
Set myself up straight (stand straight, baby)

PIECES STILL GOOD

no more of that spoon feed
no more greed
no more nothing
there'll just be nothing left
nothing left at all.

When my friends become my enemies
and my enemies start grinning
at me,
then I finally realize it's time
I better see what I didn't see.
Take everything I have
it's nothing anyway.
Just trying to get things straight
but I must admit,
it might be too late.
Lord knows it doesn't matter
I'll just go where there's sunshine,
that's what matter, at least for now.
I know that's what matter for now,
Anyhow.

Even though I may be down
it was a nice day today
I told him that and
he heard me
loud and clear
thanks for listening always
Lord, no matter how big a fool I may be

LIVE AND LEARN

just call me "big fool", that's sort of like "big foot",
but not quite exactly.

So Lord, I am your son,
and my father's son
and no son can ask for more than that
I stand, happy, Lord, and grateful
nothing, and no one has ever been treated better
Thank you.

Trying so hard Lord
to get to the top
despite those stop signs
that all say stop.
Why do they all have to say the same thing?

I've been running red lights
and they're ready to hang me
seems like a fight
and they're all ready to bang me.

Lord knows I'm trying hard
but sometimes they don't give a damn how hard
you try
they burn you anyway.

I don't mind the heat
but not from within
must stand on my feet.
Bobby, will you protect me

or is it me and the pup
and the snow and nothing else
no nothing else left at all
if this is the case
then let me know.
If not then I'll see you at the top
of the stairs,
if yes
then it's you who will be climbing
dividing line
summertime
I feel fine
favors,
no favors
I'm not free for no one,
just can't do it
I just can't do it
Don't you know that I just can't do it…

I know I can do it
I know I can do it
Don't you know that I can do it.

Hi puppy, you bummed out dog,
left me here on the rug
flyin' hard

living hard
too hard

Pup, I'll take care of you I promise
that I will
these days I spend alone now,

LIVE AND LEARN

these days you spend alone
you'll be rewarded for them.
In the very near future, I promise you that big nose
did I get my 4 kisses today, that's it,
I get 8 when I come home tonight.

PIECES STILL GOOD

www.ingramcontent.com/pod-product-compliance
Lightning Source LLC
Chambersburg PA
CBHW052020290426
44112CB00014B/2308